TITUS MINI KNITS

CW00542324

We've always been proud of our Titus yarn – its unique blend of Wensleydale, Bluefaced Leicester and British Alpaca is something that so many of our customers love, and the beautiful palette of shades is instantly evocative of our Yorkshire surroundings.

We've loved introducing the yarn to our customers with fun, one or two skein projects and this, combined with our passion to showcase new British design talent, has led us to bring together this collection of patterns.

There is an awful lot of love involved in this book. From creating the yarn in the first place to share with you, our customers; from the designers conjuring up beautiful patterns for you to be inspired by; and from the whole team here at **baa ram ewe** who have all contributed to making this book. We hope you feel that love as you work your way through, creating these wonderful projects.

Verity & Jo

baa ram ewe

JANUARY MITTS

by William Nelson

ABBREVIATIONS

DPN(s)	Double pointed needle(s)
k	Knit
k2tog	Knit 2 together
Knot	(k1, p1, k1, p1, k1) all in the same stitch, then pass the 4th, 3rd, 2nd and 1st of the newly created stitches over the last stitch made
m	Marker
m1	Make one
p	Purl
patt	Pattern
pm	Place marker
rep	Repeat
rm	Remove marker
rnd	Round
ssk	Slip first and second stitches knitwise one at a time, insert tip of left needle into front of these two stitches then knit together in this position.
st	Stitch
tbl	Through back loop
yo	Yarn over

YARN

baa ram ewe Titus, shade: White Rose; 1 x 100g skein

NEEDLES

2.5mm (UK13-12 / US1-2) DPNs or 80cm (32") circular needle for magic loop

TENSION

30 sts x 38 rows = 10cm / 4" measured over stocking stitch

OTHER SUPPLIES

Stitch markers

SIZE

One size, to fit adult, short and long lengths. 18cm / 7" circumference with 17 (19)cm / 6.5 (7.5)" length

PATTERN: LEFT MITT

Cast on 54 sts, divide over dpns. Join to work in the rnd, being careful not to twist. Pm to mark beg of rnd
Rnd 1: *P1, k1tbl; rep from * to end. Rep rnd 1 13 more times.

Short version: Skip to Rnd 21

Rnd 15: K2, [p1, k1tbl] twice, p1, work row 1 of charted lace patt across next 19 sts, [p1, k1tbl] twice, p1, k to end of rnd.
Rnd 16: K2, [p1, k1tbl] twice, p1, work next row of lace patt, [p1, k1tbl] twice, p1, k to end of rnd.
Rep this rnd 4 more times.

Rnd 21: K2, [p1, k1tbl] twice, p1, work row 1 (7) of lace patt across next 19 sts, [p1, k1tbl] twice, p1, k21, pm, m1, k2, m1. (56 sts)
Rnd 22: K2, [p1, k1tbl] twice, p1, work next row of lace patt, [p1, k1tbl] twice, p1, k to end of rnd.
Rep this rnd twice more.

Rnd 25: K2, [p1, k1tbl] twice, p1, work next row of lace patt, [p1, k1tbl] twice, p1, [k to m, m1] twice. (58 sts)
Work these last 4 rnds 6 more times.
Work rnd 22 once more. (70 sts)

DIVIDE FOR THUMB

Rnd 51: K2, [p1, k1tbl] twice, p1, work next row of lace patt, [p1, k1tbl] twice, p1, k to m, rm, place next 18 sts onto waste yarn for thumb, cast on 6 sts, rejoin to work in the rnd (58 sts)
Rnd 52: K2, [p1, k1tbl] twice, p1, work next row of lace patt, [p1, k1tbl] twice, p1, k to end of rnd.
Rep this rnd 8 (12) more times.

Next rnd: *P1, k1tbl; rep from * to end. Rep this rnd 9 times more, cast off.

THUMB

Pick up 6 sts from base of the 6 sts that were cast on in rnd 51, then transfer the sts from the waste yarn back onto double pointed needles, join to work in the rnd. (24sts)
Next rnd: *K1tbl, p1; rep from * to end of rnd. Rep this rnd 7 times more, cast off.

PATTERN: RIGHT MITT

Cast on 54 sts, divide over dpns. Join to work in the rnd, being careful not to twist. Pm to mark beg of rnd.
Rnd 1: * K1tbl, p1; rep from * to end. Rep rnd 1 13 more times.

Short version: Skip to Rnd 21.

Rnd 15: K23, pm, [p1, k1tbl] twice, p1, work row 1 of charted lace patt across next 19 sts, [p1, k1tbl] twice, p1, k2.
Rnd 16: K to m, [p1, k1tbl] twice, p1, work next row of lace patt, [p1, k1tbl] twice, p1, k2.
Rep this rnd 4 more times.

Rnd 21: M1, k2, m1, pm, k to m, [p1, k1tbl] twice, p1, work row 1 (7) of lace patt across next 19 sts, [p1, k1tbl] twice, p1, k2. (56 sts)
Rnd 22: K to 2nd marker, [p1, k1tbl] twice, p1, work next row of lace patt, [p1, k1tbl] twice, p1, k2.
Rep this rnd twice more.

Rnd 25: M1, k to m, m1, k to m, [p1, k1tbl] twice, p1, work next row of lace patt, [p1, k1tbl] twice, p1, k2. (58 sts)
Work these last 4 rnds 6 more times.
Work Rnd 22 once more. (70 sts).

DIVIDE FOR THUMB

Rnd 51: Place next 18 sts onto waste yarn for thumb, rm, cast on 6 sts, rejoin to work in the rnd, k to m, [p1, k1tbl] twice, p1, work next row of lace patt, [p1, k1tbl] twice, p1, k2. (58 sts)

Rnd 52: K to m, [p1, k1tbl] twice, p1, work next row of lace patt, [p1, k1tbl] twice, p1, k2.
Rep this rnd 8 (12) more times.

Next rnd: *K1tbl, p1; rep from * to end.
Rep this rnd 9 times more, cast off.

THUMB

Work as for left mitt.

FINISHING

Weave in loose ends. Wet block using the immersion method and pin out to dry. The openwork panel on the back of the hand should be well stretched both horizontally and vertically to open it up. Try to avoid stretching the rib.

HINTS AND TIPS

The sample mitt pictured is worked with a tubular cast on and cast off, but any reasonably elastic cast on/cast off will suffice.

If using a tubular cast on, work the knit stitches through the back loops on the right side preparatory rows to match the ribbing on the rest of the cuff.

LACE PATTERN CHART

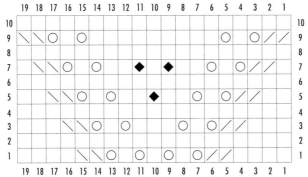

KEY

☐	Knit
○	Yarn over
╱	K2tog
╲	SSK
◆	Knot

ABBREVIATIONS

beg	Beginning
inc	Increase(d)
k	Knit
k2tog	knit two together
kfb	Knit through front and back of same stitch
p	Purl
patt	Pattern
pm	Place marker
rep	Repeat
rm	Remove marker
sm	Slip marker
ssk	Slip one knitwise, slip one purlwise, knit these two slipped stiches together
st(s)	Stitch(es)
tbl	Through the back loop
yo	Yarn over

YARN

baa ram ewe Titus, shade: Bantam;
1 (1, 1, 2, 2, 2) x 100g skein(s)

NEEDLES

3.75mm (UK 9 / US 5) circular needle,
80cm (32") length

TENSION

23 sts x 44 rows = 10cm / 4" measured
over Gull Lace pattern

OTHER SUPPLIES

Stitch markers x 6

FEBRUARY SHRUG

by Alison Moreton

SIZES

XS (S, M, L, XL, 2XL)

FITTING NOTES

The Gull Lace pattern is stretchy and the shrug is designed to fit with negative ease across the back. It is recommended you choose your size based on upper arm measurement as the armholes do not stretch.

To fit upper arm circumference:
25 (26, 28, 30.5, 34.5, 39.5) cm / 9¾ (10¼, 11, 12, 13½, 15½) in

To fit approx bust size:
71-76 (81.5-86.5, 91.5-96.5, 101.5 -106.5, 112-117, 122-127) cm / 28-30 (32-34, 36-38, 40-42, 44-46, 48-50) in

PATTERN

Cast on 82 (82, 103, 103, 124, 124) sts. Knit 6 rows.

Set-up Row (RS): K1, pm, k19 (19, 26, 26, 33, 33), pm, k1, pm, k40 (40, 47, 47, 54, 54), pm, k1, pm, k19 (19, 26, 26, 33, 33), pm, k1.

Next Row (WS): [K1, sm, kfb, k to 1 st before marker, kfb, sm] 3 times, k1. 88 (88, 109, 109, 130, 130) sts

Row 1 (RS): [K1, sm, working from the Chart or Written Instructions, work Gull Lace patt to next marker, sm] 3 times, k1.

Row 2 (WS and all following WS rows): Purl.

Rep rows 1 and 2 working the next row of the Gull Lace patt until one 32 row rep of the chart has been completed. 130 (130, 151, 151, 172, 172) sts

CONTINUE AS FOLLOWS FOR YOUR SIZE:

Size XS only: Beg with row 5 of lace patt, work as set to end of row 24 of Gull Lace patt. 20 rows worked. 160 sts

Size S only: Beg with row 5 of lace patt, work as set to end of row 32 of Gull Lace patt. 28 rows worked. 172 sts

Sizes M (L, XL, 2XL) only:
Beg with row 5 of lace patt, work as set to end of row 32 of Gull Lace patt, then starting with row 5 again, work to end of row 8 (16, 20, 28). 32 (40, 44, 52) rows worked. 199 (211, 238, 250) sts

ALL SIZES AGAIN

Knit 2 rows.

Next Row (RS): [K1, sm, kfb, k to 1 st before marker, kfb, sm] 3 times, k1. 166 (178, 205, 217, 244, 256) sts
Knit 5 rows.

SEPARATE BODY AND SLEEVES:

Next Row (RS): K1, rm, k1, cast off next 46 (50, 59, 63, 72, 76) sts to marker, rm, cast off 1 more st, rm, k to next marker, rm, k1, rm, k1, cast off next 46 (50, 59, 63, 72, 76) sts to marker, rm, cast off 1 more st. 66 (70, 85, 89, 98, 102) sts

Next row (WS): K1, using the backwards loop method, cast on 23 (23, 21, 23, 23, 27) sts for underarm, k across back sts, cast on 23 (23, 21, 23, 23, 27) sts for underarm, k1, pm, pick up and k42 (46, 48, 52, 54, 58) sts along diagonal front edge. 154 (162, 175, 187, 198, 214) sts

Next row: K to end of row, pm, pick up and k42 (46, 48, 52, 54, 58) sts along diagonal front edge. 196 (208, 223, 239, 252, 272) sts
Knit 3 rows.

Next Row: [K to 1 st before m, kfb, sm, kfb] twice, k to end. 4 sts inc
Rep last 4 rows a further 4 times. 216 (228, 243, 259, 272, 292) sts
Knit 3 rows.

Cast off using your preferred stretchy method. We suggest the following: K2, *place left needle into the front of both sts on right needle, k2tog tbl, k1; rep from * to end finishing with k2tog tbl.
Weave in ends. Block gently to open the lace pattern.

WRITTEN INSTRUCTIONS: GULL LACE PATTERN

Row 1 (RS): *K1, k2tog, yo, k1, yo, ssk, k1; rep from * to end.
Row 2 (WS and all following WS rows): Purl.
Row 3: *K2tog, yo, k3, yo, ssk; rep from * to end.
Row 5: Yo, *k1, k2tog, yo, k1, yo, ssk, k1; rep from * to end, yo.
Row 7: K1, *k2tog, yo, k3, yo, ssk; rep from * to last st, k1.
Row 9: Yo, k1, *k1, k2tog, yo, k1, yo, ssk, k1; rep from * to last st, k1, yo.
Row 11: Yo, ssk, *k2tog, yo, k3, yo, ssk; rep from * to last 2 sts, k2tog, yo.
Row 13: Yo, k2, *k1, k2tog, yo, k1, yo, ssk, k1; rep from * to last 2 sts, k2, yo.
Row 15: K1, yo, ssk, *k2tog, yo, k3, yo, ssk; rep from * to last 3 sts, k2tog, yo, k1.
Row 17: Yo, k3, *k1, k2tog, yo, k1, yo, ssk, k1; rep from * to last 3 sts, k3, yo.

Row 19: K2, yo, ssk, *k2tog, yo, k3, yo, ssk; rep from * to last 4 sts, k2tog, yo, k2.
Row 21: Yo, k1, yo, ssk, k1, *k1, k2tog, yo, k1, yo, ssk, k1; rep from * to last 4 sts, k1, k2tog, yo, k1, yo.
Row 23: K3, yo, ssk, *k2tog, yo, k3, yo, ssk; rep from * to last 5 sts, k2tog, yo, k3.
Row 25: Yo, k2, yo, ssk, k1, *k1, k2tog, yo, k1, yo, ssk, k1; rep from * to last 5 sts, k1, k2tog, yo, k2, yo.
Row 27: K4, yo, ssk, *k2tog, yo, k3, yo, ssk; rep from * to last 6 sts, k2tog, yo, k4.
Row 29: Yo, k2tog, yo, k1, yo, ssk, k1, *k1, k2tog, yo, k1, yo, ssk, k1; rep from * to last 6 sts, k1, k2tog, yo, k1, yo, ssk, yo.
Row 31: *K2tog, yo, k3, yo, ssk; rep from * to end.

GULL LACE CHART

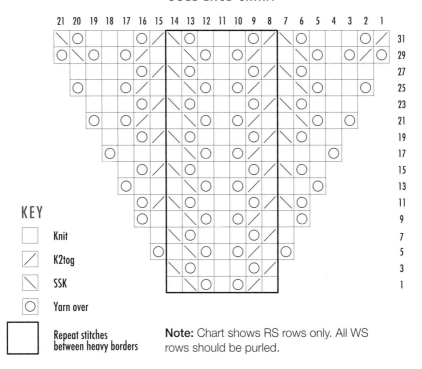

KEY

☐	Knit
╱	K2tog
╲	SSK
◯	Yarn over
⬜	Repeat stitches between heavy borders

Note: Chart shows RS rows only. All WS rows should be purled.

SCHEMATIC

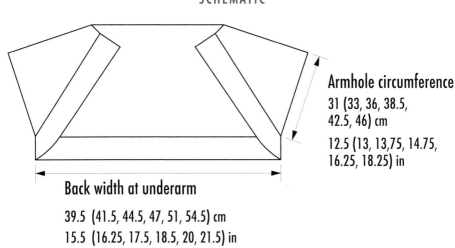

Armhole circumference

31 (33, 36, 38.5, 42.5, 46) cm

12.5 (13, 13,75, 14.75, 16.25, 18.25) in

Back width at underarm

39.5 (41.5, 44.5, 47, 51, 54.5) cm

15.5 (16.25, 17.5, 18.5, 20, 21.5) in

BARLEY SUGAR

by Anna Ellis

ABBREVIATIONS

1x1 rib	K1, p1 ribbing
beg	Begin/beginning
cm	Centimetres
CN	Cable needle
C4B	Cable 4 back: sl 2st to CN, hold in back, k2 from LH needle, k2 from CN
dec	Decrease
DPN(s)	Double pointed needles
foll	Following
k	Knit
kfb	Knit through front and back of same stitch
LH	Left hand
p	Purl
patt	Pattern
p2tog	Purl two together
pm	Place marker
rem	Remaining
rep	Repeat
rnd	Round
sl	Slip stitch
st	Stitch
wyib	With yarn in back
wyif	With yarn in front

YARN

baa ram ewe Titus, shade: Filey; 2 x 100g skeins (hat and mitts each need one skein)

NEEDLES

Set of 2.5mm (UK13-12 / US1-2) DPNs
Set of 2.75mm (UK12 / US2) DPNs

TENSION

30 sts x 32 rows = 10cm/ 4" measured over Barley Sugar cable pattern

OTHER SUPPLIES

Stitch marker; Cable needle; Tapestry needle

SIZES

Hat

Size 1: 54-57cm / 21.25-22.5" head circumference

Size 2: 57-60cm / 22.5-23.5" head circumference

Mitts

Size 1: 15-20cm / 6-7.75" at wrist with 0-5cm / 0-2" negative ease

Size 2: 18-23cm / 7-9" at wrist with 0-5cm / 0-2" negative ease

PATTERN: HAT

With smaller needles, cast on 112 (120) sts. Join to work in the rnd, being careful not to twist. PM for beg of rnd.

BRIM

Work in Border Patt as foll:
Rnd 1: K1 *sl1 wyif, k3; rep from * to last 3 sts, sl1wyif, k2.
Rnd 2: *P3, sl1 wyib; rep from * to end.
Rep these 2 rnds until work measures 5cm from cast on edge.

BODY

Change to larger needles.
Next rnd: Kfb in every st to end. 224 (240) sts.
Purl four rnds.

Beg Barley Sugar Cable patt using chart or written instructions as follows:
Rnd 1: *K4, p4; rep from * to end.
Rnds 2-4: As for rnd 1.
Rnd 5: *C4B, p4; rep from * to end.
Rnds 6-9: As for rnds 2-5.
Rnds 10-13: As for rnds 1-4.
Rnds 14-16: Purl 3 rnds.
Rnd 17: *P4, k4; rep from * to end.
Rnds 18-20: As for rnd 17.
Rnd 21: *P4, C4B; rep from * to end.
Rnds 22-25: As for rnds 18-21.
Rnds 26-29: As for rnds 17-20.
Rnds 30-32: Purl 3 rnds.
Rep rnds 1 to 32 once more.

CROWN

Rnd 1: *P6, p2tog; rep from * to end of rnd. 196 (210) sts
Rnd 2 and all even rnds: Purl.
Rnd 3: *P5, p2tog; rep from * to end of rnd. 168 (180) sts
Rnd 5: *P4, p2tog; rep from * to end of rnd. 140 (150) sts

Rnd 7: *P3, p2tog; rep from * to end of rnd. 112 (120) sts
Rnd 9: *P2, p2tog; rep from * to end of rnd. 84 (90) sts
Rnd 11: *P1, p2tog; rep from * to end of rnd. 56 (60) sts
Rnd 13: *P2tog; rep from * to end. 28 (30) sts
Next rnd: Purl.
Rep these last two rnds once more.

Break yarn leaving a long tail, thread through rem 14 (15) sts and fasten off. Weave in ends and lightly steam block.

PATTERN: MITTS

MAKE TWO THE SAME
With smaller needles cast on 64 (72) sts. Join to work in the rnd, being careful not to twist. PM for beg of rnd.

CUFF

Work in 1x1 rib as foll:
Rnd 1: *K1, p1; rep from * to end.
Rep this rnd 9 more times.

BODY

Change to larger needles.
Purl 3 rnds.
Beg Barley Sugar Cable patt as for Hat.
Work rnds 1-32 twice.
Change to smaller needles and work 12cm in Border Patt as for Hat.

THUMB HOLE
Next rnd: Cast off 8 (10) sts, *k1, p1; rep from * to end. 56 (62) sts
Next rnd: Cast on 8 (10) sts using backwards loop then work in 1x1 rib as established to end. 64 (72) sts

Work in 1x1 rib as established for 2cm. Cast off.
Weave in ends and lightly steam block.

KEY

☐	Knit
●	Purl
⧖	C4b

BARLEY SUGAR CABLE CHART

```
  8  7  6  5  4  3  2  1
                           32
                           31
                           30
                           29
                           28
                           27
                           26
                           25
                           24
                           23
                           22
                           21
                           20
                           19
                           18
                           17
                           16
                           15
                           14
                           13
                           12
                           11
                           10
                            9
                            8
                            7
                            6
                            5
                            4
                            3
                            2
                            1
  8  7  6  5  4  3  2  1
```

HINTS AND TIPS

The Barley Sugar Cable pattern will create quite a springy, corrugated effect when first knitted. This effect will lessen with blocking – lightly steam block to retain the texture or block more vigorously if you want a flatter fabric; note that this will increase the ease, especially for the upper part of the mitts.

Both the hat and mitts can be worked using circular needles using the 'magic loop' technique instead of DPNs. Use a 60cm (24") circular needle for the hat.

For the mitts, you may find it easier to use two shorter circular needles. If you would prefer armwarmers rather than mitts, simply omit the thumb hole rnds and work in 1x1 rib to end.

ABBREVIATIONS

beg	Beginning
cm	Centimetres
dec	Decrease
k	Knit
m	Marker
m1l	From the front, lift the strand between stitches onto left needle and knit tbl
m1r	From the front lift the strand between stitches onto left needle and knit
m1p	From the front lift the strand between stitches onto left needle and purl tbl
p	Purl
PM	Place marker
tbl	Through back loop
sm	Slip marker
ssk	Slip one knitwise, slip one purlwise, knit two slipped stiches together

YARN

baa ram ewe Titus, shade: Endeavour; 1 x 100g skein (40g per pair of mitts, 20g each mitt)

NEEDLES

Set of 2.5mm (UK13-12/US1-2) DPNs
One 2.75mm (UK12 / US2) needle for casting off

TENSION

32sts x 40rows = 10cm / 4" measured over stocking stitch

OTHER SUPPLIES

Stitch markers; Tapestry needle; Scrap yarn

SIZE

17 (19, 22)cm / 6½ (7½, 8½)" hand diameter
22cm / 8½" long

PATTERN: LEFT MITT

CUFF

With 2.5mm needles and the Old Norwegian Cast On (see Special Instructions), cast on 46 (54, 62) sts and join to work in the rnd, being careful not to twist. PM to mark beg of rnd.

Rib rnd: *K1, p1; rep from * to end of rnd. Rep this rnd until cuff measures 2cm.

Next rnd: M1l, *k1, p1; rep from * to end of rnd. 47 (55, 63) sts **

WRIST

Rnd 1: K4 (6, 8), p1, k5, p1, k5, p1, k4 (6, 8), p1, k1, ssk, k20 (24, 28), m1l, k1, p1.

Rnd 2: K4 (6, 8), p1, k5, p1, k5, p1, k4 (6,8), p1, k24 (28, 32), p1.

Rnd 3: K4 (6, 8), p1, k5, p1, k5, p1, k4 (6,8), p1, k24 (28, 32), p1.

Rep these last 3 rnds until mitt measures 7.5 (9, 9)cm/3 (3.5, 3.5)" from cast on (or desired length) ending after rnd 2.

Next rnd: [K10 (12, 14), p1] twice, k24 (28, 32), p1.

THUMB SET-UP

Rnd 1: K10 (12, 14), p1, k10 (12, 14), p twice in the same st, placing 2 st markers between sts, k1, ssk, k20 (24, 28), m1l, k1, p1. 48 (56, 64) sts

Rnd 2: [K10 (12, 14), p1] twice, sm, m1p, sm, p1, k24 (28, 32), p1. 49 (57, 65) sts

Rnd 3: [K10 (12, 14), p1] twice, sm, p1, sm, k24 (28, 32), p1.

Rnd 4: [K10 (12, 14), p1] twice, sm, m1r, p1, m1l, sm, p1, k1, ssk, k20 (24, 28), m1, k1, p1. 51 (59, 67) sts

Rnd 5: [K10 (12, 14), p1] twice, sm, k1, p1 (this st will be referred to as centre st), k1, slip marker, p1, k24 (28, 32), p1.

Rnd 6: As for rnd 5.

Rnd 7: [K10 (12, 14), p1] twice, sm, m1r, k to centre st, p centre st, k to m, m1l, sm, p1, k1, ssk, k20 (24, 28), m1, k1 p1.

STAYSAIL
REVERSIBLE MITTS

by Graeme Knowles-Miller

Rnd 8: [K10 (12, 14), p1] twice, sm, k to centre st, p centre st, k to m, sm, p1, k24 (28, 32), p1.

Rnd 9: As for rnd 8. 69 (77, 85) sts

Next rnd: [K10 (12, 14), p1] twice, sm, k to centre st, p centre st, k to m, sm, transfer these last 21 sts between markers to scrap yarn and remove markers, p1, k1, ssk, k20 (24, 28), k1, m1, p1. 48 (56, 64) sts

PALM

Set up rnd: K10 (12, 14), p1, k10 (12, 14), p2tog, k1, ssk, k20 (24, 28), m1l, k1, p1. 47 (55, 63) sts

Next rnd: [K10 (12, 14), p1] twice, k24 (28, 32), p1.

Work this rnd once more.

Next rnd: [K10 (12, 14), p1] twice, k1, ssk, k20 (24, 28), m1, k1, p1.

Next rnd: [K10 (12, 14), p1] twice, k24 (28, 32), p1.

Work this rnd once more.

Rep these last 3 rnds until mitt measures 17.5 (19,19)cm/7 (7.5, 7.5)" from cast on edge or 1.5cm/0.5" less than desired length.

Next rnd: *K1, p1; rep from * to last st, k1, m1p. 48 (56, 64) sts

Next rnd: *K1, p1; rep from * to end of rnd. Work this rnd until rib measures 1.5cm/0.5". Cast off using 2.75 mm needle.

THUMB

Using 2.5mm needles, pick up 21 sts held on scrap yarn and pick up 1 st from palm edge, re-join yarn and pm for beg of rnd. 22 sts

Next rnd: *P1, k1; rep from * to end of rnd. Repeat this rnd until thumb measures 2.5cm/1" or desired length. Cast off using 2.75 mm needle. Weave in ends invisibly and block to shape.

PATTERN: RIGHT MITT

Work cuff as for left mitt to **

WRIST

Rnd 1: K1, m1r, k20 (24, 28), k2tog, k1, p1, k4 (6, 8), p1, k5, p1, k5, p1, k4 (6, 8), p1.

Rnd 2: K24 (28, 32), p1, k4 (6, 8), p1, k5, p1, k5, p1, k4 (6, 8), p1.

Rnd 3: K24 (28, 32), p1, k4 (6, 8), p1, k5, p1, k5, p1, k4 (6, 8), p1.

Rep these last three rnds until mitt measures 7.5 (9, 9)cm/3 (3.5, 3.5)" from cast on or desired length, ending after rnd 2.

Next rnd: K24 (28, 32), p1, [k10 (12, 14), p1] twice.

THUMB SET-UP

Rnd 1: K1, m1r, k20 (24, 28), k2tog, k1, p twice in the same st, placing 2 st markers between sts, [k10 (12, 14), p1] twice. 48 (56, 64) sts

Rnd 2: K24 (28, 32), p1, sm, m1p, sm, p1, [k10 (12, 14), p1] twice. 49 (57, 65) sts

Rnd 3: K24 (28, 32), p1, sm, p1, sm, [k10 (12,1 4), p1] twice.

Rnd 4: K1, m1r, k20 (24, 28), k2tog, k1, p1, sm, m1r, p1, m1l, sm, p1, [k10 (12, 14), p1] twice. 51 (59, 67) sts

Rnd 5: K24 (28, 32), p1, sm, k1, p1 (this st will be referred to as centre st), k1, sm, p1, [k10 (12, 14), p1] twice.

Rnd 6: As for rnd 5.

Rnd 7: K1, m1r, k20 (24, 28), k2tog, k1, p1, sm, m1r, k to centre st, p centre st, k to m, m1l, sm, p1, [k10 (12, 14), p1] twice.

Rnd 8: K24 (28, 32), p1, sm, k to centre st, p centre st, k to m, sm, p1, [k10 (12, 14), p1] twice.

Rnd 9: As for Rnd 8.

Work these last 3 rnds seven more times. Work rnds 7 and 8 once more. 69 (77, 85) sts

Next rnd: K24 (28, 32), p1, sm,
k to centre st, p centre st, k to m, sm,
transfer these last 21 sts between
markers to scrap yarn and remove
markers, p1, [k10 (12, 14), p1] twice.

PALM
Set up rnd: K1, m1r, k20 (24, 28), k2tog,
K1, p2tog, [k10 (12, 14), p1] twice.
Next rnd: K24 (28, 32), p1, [k10 (12, 14),
p1] twice.
Work this rnd once more.
Next rnd: K1, m1r, k20 (24, 28), k2tog,
p1, [k10 (12, 14), p1] twice.
Next rnd: K24 (28, 32), p1, [k10 (12, 14),
p1] twice.
Work this rnd once more.

Rep these last 3 rnds until mitt measures
17.5 (19,19)cm/7 (7.5, 7.5)" from cast
on edge or 1.5cm/0.5" less than desired
length.
Next rnd: *K1, p1; rep from * to last st,
k1, m1p. 48 (56, 64) sts
Next rnd: *K1, p1; rep from * to end of rnd.
Work this rnd until rib measures
1.5cm/0.5". Cast off using 2.75mm
needle.

THUMB
Work thumb as for left mitt.

Cast off using 2.75mm needle.
Weave in ends. Block to shape.

SPECIAL INSTRUCTIONS
The Old Norwegian Cast On gives a
stretchy edge. This cast on method is
also known as German Twisted Cast
On. Use any stretchy cast on method
you prefer. If you're not sure how to
do the Old Norwegian Cast On, try
popping it in your favourite search
engine online.

HINTS AND TIPS
If you find it difficult to keep track of the
centre stitch in the thumb increases,
mark it with a locking stitch marker and
move the marker up every rnd.

MAY COWL

by Sarah Alderson

ABBREVIATIONS
UK crochet terms used throughout

ch	Chain
ch-sp	Chain-space
dc	Double crochet
dc2tog	Double crochet 2 stitches together
rep	Repeat
RS	Right side
st(s)	Stitch(es)
tr	Treble crochet
WS	Wrong side

YARN
baa ram ewe Titus, shade: Chevin;
2 x 100g skeins for each size

HOOK
3.5mm (UK 9 / US E/4)

GAUGE
19 sts x 19 rows = 10cm / 4" over dc,
after blocking.

OTHER SUPPLIES
7 x 1cm / ½" buttons

SIZE
S (M, L, XL, XXL) Shown in size S
Depth: 46cm / 18"
Length: 114 (127, 140, 152, 165)cm
/ 45 (50, 55, 60, 65)"

PATTERN

Set-up row: Make 218 (242, 266, 290, 314) ch, 1dc in second ch from hook, dc to end, turn. 217 (241, 265, 289, 313) sts

Row 1 (RS): 1ch, 1dc, *6ch, miss 5 sts, 1dc in next st; rep from * to end, turn.

Row 2: 4ch (counts as first tr and 1ch-sp), 2tr in top of first dc, 1ch, 1dc in ch-sp, *1ch, [2tr, 1ch, 2tr] in next st (cluster made), 1ch, 1dc in next ch-sp; rep from * to last ch-sp, 1ch, [2tr, 1ch, 1tr] in last dc, turn.

Row 3: *1ch, 1dc in cluster ch-sp, 1ch, [2tr, 1ch, 2tr] in next cluster ch-sp, 1ch, 1dc in ch-sp of next cluster; rep from * to end, turn.

Row 4: 1ch, 1dc, *6ch, 1dc in ch-sp of next cluster; rep from * to last cluster, 3ch, 1tr in dc, turn.

Row 5: 1ch, 1dc in top of tr, *6ch, 1dc in next ch-sp; rep from * to end, turn.

Row 6: *6ch, 1dc in next ch-sp; rep from * to last ch-sp, 3ch, 1tr in last dc, turn.

Rows 7-8: Rep Rows 5-6.

Row 9: 1ch, 1dc in top of tr, *1ch, [2tr, 1ch, 2tr] in next dc, 1ch, 1dc in next ch-sp; rep from * to end, turn.

Row 10: *6ch, 1dc in ch-sp of cluster; rep from * to last cluster ch-sp, 3ch, 1tr in dc, turn.

Rows 11-12: Rep Rows 9-10.

Row 13: 1ch, 1dc in top of tr, *6ch, 1dc in next ch-sp; rep from * to end, turn.

Row 14: *6ch, 1dc in next ch-sp; rep from * to last ch-sp, 3ch, 1tr in dc, turn.

Rows 15-16: Rep Rows 13-14.

Row 17: 1ch, 1dc in top of tr, *1ch, [2tr, 1ch, 2tr] in next dc, 1ch, 1dc in next ch-sp; rep from * to end, turn.

Row 18: 4ch (counts as first tr and 1ch-sp), 2tr in dc, 1ch, 1dc in ch-sp of cluster, *1ch, [2tr, 1ch, 2tr] in next dc, 1ch, 1dc in ch-sp of cluster; rep from * to last ch-space, 1ch, [2tr, 1ch, 1tr] in last dc, turn.

Row 19: 1ch, 1dc in ch-sp of cluster, *1ch, [2tr, 1ch, 2tr] in next dc, 1ch, 1dc in next ch-sp; rep from * to end, turn.

Row 20: Rep Row 19.

Row 21: 1ch, 1dc, *6ch, 1dc in ch-sp of cluster; rep from * to end, turn.

Row 22: Rep Row 3.

Row 23: Rep Row 20.

Row 24: Rep Row 19.

Fasten off.

With RS facing, rejoin yarn in first dc of row 2.

Rep rows 1-24, but do not fasten off.

Turn and continue as follows:

BORDER

Row 1 (RS): 1ch, work 100dc along edge st of cowl, turn. (100 sts)

Row 2 (WS): 1ch, dc to end, turn.

Row 3: 1ch, dc2tog, dc to last 2 sts, dc2tog, turn. (98 sts)

Row 4: 1ch, *1dc, 1ch, miss 2 sts, [2tr, 1ch, 2tr] in next dc, 1ch, miss 2 sts; rep from * to 8 sts before end, 1dc, 1ch, miss 2 sts, [2tr, 1ch, 2tr] in next dc, 1ch, miss 2 sts, dc2tog.

Fasten off.

BUTTONHOLE BAND

With RS facing rejoin yarn at other end of cowl.

Row 1 (RS): 1ch, 100dc along edge sts of cowl, turn. 100 sts

Row 2 (WS) (Buttonhole row): 1ch, 13dc, 2ch, miss 2 sts, *10dc, 2ch, miss 2 sts; rep from * to 13 sts before end, 13dc, turn.

Row 3: 1ch, dc2tog, dc to last 2 sts, dc2tog. 98 sts

Row 4: 1ch, *1dc, 1ch, miss 2 sts, [2tr, 1ch, 2tr] in next dc, 1ch; rep from * to 8 sts before end, 1dc, 1ch, miss 2 sts, [2tr, 1ch, 2tr] in next dc, 1ch, dc2tog.
Fasten off.

FINISHING

Weave in the loose ends and block to measurements.
Stitch buttons in place aligning them with the buttonholes.

JUNE SHAWL

by Patricia Martin

ABBREVIATIONS

cm	Centimetres
g st	Garter stitch
k	Knit
k2tog	Knit two together
p	Purl
rep	Repeat
RS	Right side
sk2p	Slip stitch, knit two together, pass slipped stitch over
ssk	Slip one knitwise, slip one purlwise, knit two slipped stitches together
sts	Stitches
WS	Wrong side
Yo	Yarn over

YARN

baa ram ewe Titus, shade: Bramley Baths; 2 x 100g skeins

NEEDLES

4mm (UK8 / US6) 80cm / 32" circular needle or longer

GAUGE

20 sts x 28 rows = 10cm / 4" measured over stocking stitch

SIZE

One size, adapt by removing or adding repeats. 160cm x 45.5cm / 63" x 18"

PATTERN
With 4mm needles, cast on 259 sts.

MAIN BODY OF SHAWL
Row 1 (RS): K2, *k3, yo, k2tog, k2, yo, sk2p, yo, k2, ssk, yo, k3; rep from * to last 2 sts, k2.
Row 2 (and all WS rows): K2, p to last 2 sts, k2.
Row 3: K2, *k2, yo, k2tog, k2, yo, k1, sk2p, k1, yo, k2, ssk, yo, k2; rep from * to last 2 sts, k2.
Row 5: K2, *k1, yo, k2tog, k2, yo, k2, sk2p, k2, yo, k2, ssk, yo, k1; rep from * to last 2 sts, k2.
Row 7: K2, *k4, yo, k3, sk2p, k3, yo, k4; rep from * to last 2 sts, k2.
Row 9: K2, *k3, yo, k4, sk2p, k4, yo, k3; rep from * to last 2 sts, k2.
Row 11: K2, *k2, yo, k5, sk2p, k5, yo, k2; rep from * to last 2 sts, k2.
Row 13: K2, *k1, yo, k6, sk2p, k6, yo, k1; rep from * to last 2 sts, k2.
Row 15: K2, *k1, yo, k6, sk2p, k6, yo, k1; rep from * to last 2 sts, k2.
Row 17: K2, *k2, yo, k5, sk2p, k5, yo, k2; rep from * to last 2 sts, k2.
Row 19: K2, *k3, yo, k4, sk2p, k4, yo, k3; rep from * to last 2 sts, k2.
Row 21: K2, *k4, yo, k3, sk2p, k3, yo, k4; rep from * to last 2 sts, k2.
Row 23: K2, *k1, yo, ssk, k2, yo, k2, sk2p, k2, yo, k2, k2tog, yo, k1; rep from * to last 2 sts, k2.
Row 25: K2, *k2, yo, ssk, k2, yo, k1, sk2p, k1, yo, k2, k2tog, yo, k2; rep from * to last 2 sts, k2.
Row 27: K2, *k3, yo, ssk, k2, yo, sk2p, yo, k2, k2tog, yo, k3; rep from * to last 2 sts, k2.
Row 28 (WS): K2, p to last 2 sts, k2.
Work Rows 1-28 twice more (84 rows worked in total).

INSIDE BORDER
Work Rows 1-14 a further two times.

BORDER
Work Rows 1-8 again.
Row 29: K2, *k4, yo, k3, yo, sk2p, yo, k3, yo, k4; rep from * to last 2 sts, k2. 289 sts
Row 30 (and all WS in border): K2, p to last 2 sts, k2.
Row 31: K2, *k4, yo, k3, yo, k1, sk2p, k1, yo, k3, yo, k4; rep from * to last 2 sts, k2. 319 sts
Row 33: K2, *k4, yo, k3, yo, k2, sk2p, k2, yo, k3, yo, k4; rep from * to last 2 sts, k2. 349 sts
Row 34 (WS): K2, p to last 2 sts, k2.

Cast off loosely and weave in ends.
Wet block, stretched to 160cm x 45.5cm / 63" x 18".

HINTS AND TIPS
The way the decreases and increases work together in this pattern creates a scalloped effect at the cast-on and cast-off edges. Bear this in mind when blocking so you can emphasise the points.

You can make the shawl wider or narrower by adding or removing stitches in multiples of 17, and deeper or shallower by working more or fewer vertical repeats in the main body or inside border.

CHARTS

All WS rows are purled. Shawl is worked with 2 edge sts in g-st (not shown)

KEY

☐	Knit
Ο	Yarn over
╱	K2tog
╲	SSK
∧	SK2P
▓	No stitch

Chart 1

17	16	15	14	13	12	11	10	9	8	7	6	5	4	3	2	1	
			Ο	╱			Ο	∧	Ο			╲	Ο				14
		Ο	╱			Ο		∧		Ο			╲	Ο			13
	Ο	╱			Ο			∧			Ο			╲	Ο		12
				Ο				∧				Ο					11
			Ο					∧			Ο						10
		Ο						∧		Ο							9
	Ο							∧							Ο		8
	Ο							∧							Ο		7
		Ο						∧					Ο				6
			Ο					∧				Ο					5
				Ο				∧			Ο						4
	Ο	╲			Ο			∧			Ο			╱	Ο		3
		Ο	╲			Ο		∧	Ο					╱	Ο		2
			Ο	╲			Ο	∧	Ο				╱	Ο			1
17	16	15	14	13	12	11	10	9	8	7	6	5	4	3	2	1	

Chart 2

23	22	21	20	19	18	17	16	15	14	13	12	11	10	9	8	7	6	5	4	3	2	1	
				Ο				Ο			∧		Ο				Ο						3
▓	▓	▓			Ο					Ο	∧	Ο				Ο				▓	▓	▓	3
▓	▓	▓				Ο			Ο	Ο	∧	Ο			Ο					▓	▓	▓	2
23	22	21	20	19	18	17	16	15	14	13	12	11	10	9	8	7	6	5	4	3	2	1	

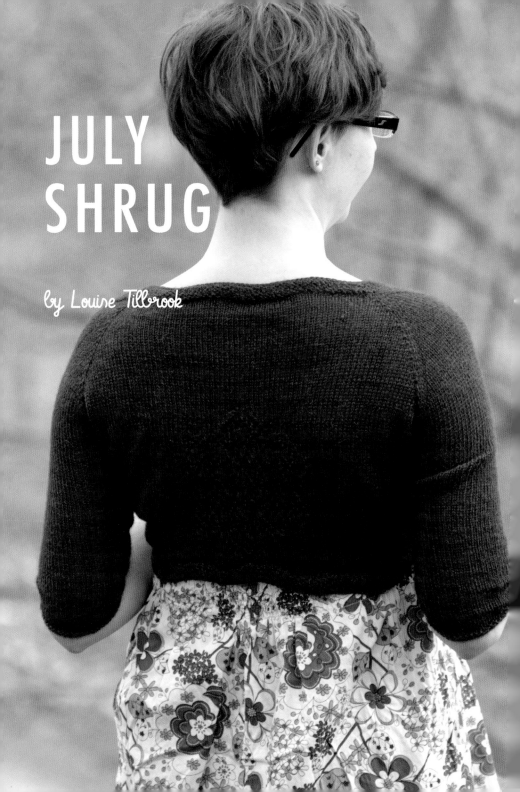

JULY
SHRUG

by Louise Tillbrook

ABBREVIATIONS

alt	Alternate
approx	Approximately
beg	Beginning
cdd	Centred double decrease: slip 2 stitches together knitwise, knit 1, pass slipped stitches over
cm	Centimetres
cont	Continue
dec	Decrease
DPN	Double pointed needle
foll	Following
G st	Garter stitch
in	Inches
inc	Increase
incl	Including
k	Knit
kfb	Knit through the front then through the back of the same stitch
k2tog	Knit two together
k3tog	knit 3 together (2 st dec)
m	Marker
p	Purl
p-wise	Purlwise
patt	Pattern
pm	Place marker
psso	Pass slipped stitch over
Raglan inc	Incs worked either side of m placed in Row 1
rep	Repeat
rm	Remove marker
rnd	Round
row	Row
RS	Right side
sk2p	Slip 1, knit 2 together, pass slipped stitch over
sl	Slip
ssk	Slip one knitwise, slip one purlwise, knit two slipped stiches together
ssp	Slip one, slip one, purl two slipped stitches together
sssk	Slip, slip, slip, k (2 st dec)
st	Stitch
St st	Stocking stitch
tbl	Through back loop
tog	Together
WS	Wrong side
yo	Yarn over

YARN
baa ram ewe Titus, shade: Bantam; 1 (2, 2) x 100g skein(s)

NEEDLES
3mm (UK11/US3) circular needle ideally 60-80cm/24-32" long
Set of 3mm (UK11/US3) DPNs or preferred needles for small circumference knitting

OTHER SUPPLIES
Stitch markers (2 being different from the others to denote the back lace panel)
Waste yarn or stitch holders

GAUGE
24 sts x 36 rows = 10cm / 4" measured over stocking stitch

SIZE
S (M, L), to fit bust 81-86 (91-96, 101-106)cm / 32-34 (36-38, 40-42)". Designed to fit with 2-4cm / 0.75-1.5" positive ease.

PATTERN

Using circular needle, cast on 55 (57,59) sts.

Set-up row: P2, pm, p2, pm, p47 (49, 51), pm, p2, pm, p2.

Row 1 (RS): [K to 1 st before m, yo, k1, sl m, yo] four times, k to end. 63, 65, 67 sts

Row 2 (WS): Purl, working all yo tbl.

Rep rows 1 and 2 18 times more until you have 207 (209, 211) sts. At this point markers are placed for the central back lace panel and front raglan incs.

BACK LACE PANEL

This is worked on the 31 sts between 2 new markers using Chart A or written directions.

Row 3 (RS): K to m, sl m, yo, k to 1 st before m, yo, k1, sl m, yo, k27 (28,29), pm, work Row 1 of lace panel, pm, k to 1st before m, yo, k1, sl m, yo, k to 1st before m, yo, k1, sl m, k to end. 213 (215, 217) sts

Row 4 (WS): Purl, working raglan inc yos tbl.

Cont in pattern as set with 6 increases on each RS row until you have completed 14 (20, 26) rows of lace panel, ending with a WS row. 249 (269, 289) sts

Separate the sleeves as foll:

Next row (RS): K21, rm, place next 54 (60, 66) sts onto waste yarn, cast on 6 sts for underarm, work as set over 99 (107, 115) sts for back, rm, place next 54 (60, 66) sts onto waste yarn, cast on 6 sts for underarm, k 21. 153 (161, 169) sts

Cont working the back lace panel with no further raglan incs until you have completed row 55 of lace panel. Then, rm and work central 31 st back panel in st st, **at the same time** work as set until body measures 5 (6.5, 8)cm/2 (2.5, 3)" from underarm to bottom.

Then work decs as foll:

Row 5: K1, ssk, work as set to last 3 sts, k2tog, k1. 151 (159, 167) sts

Row 6-8: Work as set.

Row 9: As for Row 5. 149 (157, 165) sts

Row 10: As for Row 6.

Rep Rows 5 and 6 eight more times. 133 (141,149) sts

Row 11: K1, sssk, work as set to last 4 sts, k3tog, k1. 129 (137, 145) sts

Row 12: Work as set.

Rep Rows 11 and 12 two more times. 121 (129, 137) sts

After final dec row (RS), do not turn but instead start to work border in the rnd.

BORDER WORKED IN THE RND

Pick up and k74 (83, 91) sts along right front, pick up and k55 (57, 59) sts from cast on across neck, pick up and k74 (83, 91) sts along left front, pm to mark beg of rnd. 324, (352, 378) sts

SIZES S AND L ONLY

Next rnd: Purl 1 rnd.

SIZE M ONLY

Next rnd: [Pfb, p43] 8 times. 360 sts

ALL SIZES

Rnd 1: K2tog three times, [yo, k1] six times, *k2tog six times, [yo, k1] six times; rep from * to last 6 st, k2tog three times.

Rnd 2: Purl, working all yo tbl.

Rnd 3: Knit

Rnd 4: as for Rnd 2.

Rep Rnds 1-4 once more.

Cast off loosely.

SLEEVES WORK 2
Slip held sleeve sts onto DPNs. Rejoin yarn and pick up and k 3 sts from underarm cast on, pm, pick up and k 3 sts from underarm cast on, k to m. 60 (66, 72) sts

Rnd 1: K1, ssk, k to 3 st before m, k2tog, k1. 58 (64, 70) sts

Rnd 2: Knit.

SHORT SLEEVED VERSION
K 6 more rnds, then work g st for 3 rnds (p1 rnd, k1 rnd, p1 rnd). Cast off quite firmly.

LONGER SLEEVED VERSION
Repeat dec (as Rnd 1) every 8th rnd until you have 52 (58, 64) sts then k every rnd until sleeve measures 24cm/9.5" or desired length. Work g st for 3 rnds (p1 rnd, k1 rnd, p1 rnd). Cast off quite firmly.

Weave in all ends and block gently to finished measurements.

WRITTEN LACE INSTRUCTIONS

LACE PANEL
Work WS rows – p all sts
Row 1 (RS): K13, k2tog, yo, k1 tbl, yo, ssk, k13.

Row 2 and all WS rows: Purl.

Row 3: K12, k2tog, yo, k1 tbl, k1, k1 tbl, yo, ssk, k12.

Row 5: K11, k2tog, yo, k1 tbl, k3, k1 tbl, yo, ssk, k11.

Row 7: K10, k2tog, yo, k1 tbl, k1, k2tog, yo, k2, k1 tbl, yo, ssk, k10.

Row 9: K5, k2tog, yo, k1 tbl, yo, sk2p, yo, k1 tbl, k1, k2tog, yo, k1 tbl, yo, ssk, k1, k1 tbl, yo, k3tog, yo, k1 tbl, yo, ssk, k5.

Row 11: K4, [k2tog, yo, k1 tbl, k1, k1 tbl, yo, ssk, k1] 3 times, k3.

Row 13: K3, k2tog, yo, k1 tbl, k3, k1 tbl, yo, ssk, k1, k1 tbl, yo, sk2p, yo, k1 tbl, k1, k2tog, yo, k1 tbl, k3, k1 tbl, yo, ssk, k3.

Row 15: K2, k2tog, yo, k1 tbl, k1, k2tog, yo, k2, [k1 tbl, yo, ssk, k1] twice, k2tog, yo, k1 tbl, k1, k2tog, yo, k2, k1 tbl, yo, ssk, k2.

Row 17: [K1, k2tog, yo, k1 tbl] twice, yo, [ssk, k1, k1 tbl, yo] twice, sk2p, yo, k1 tbl, k1, k2tog, yo, [k1 tbl, yo, ssk, k1] twice.

Row 19: [K2tog, yo, k1 tbl, k1] twice, [k1 tbl, yo, ssk, k1] 3 times, k2tog, yo, k1 tbl, [k1, k1 tbl, yo, ssk] twice.

Row 21: K1, k1 tbl, yo, ssk, k1, k1 tbl, yo, sk2p, yo, k1 tbl, k1, k2tog, yo, k1 tbl, yo, [ssk, k1, k1 tbl, yo] twice, sk2p, yo, k1 tbl, k1, k2tog, yo, k1 tbl, k1.

Row 23: K2, [k1 tbl, yo, ssk, k1] twice, k2tog, yo, k1 tbl, [k1, k1 tbl, yo, ssk] 4 times, k2.

Row 25: K3, k1 tbl, yo, ssk, k1, k1 tbl, yo, sk2p, yo, k1 tbl, k1, k2tog, yo, k1 tbl, yo, [ssk, k1, k1 tbl, yo] twice, sk2p, yo, k1 tbl, k3.

Row 27: K4, [k1 tbl, yo, ssk, k1] twice, k2tog, yo, k1 tbl, [k1, k1 tbl, yo, ssk] 3 times, k4.

Row 29: K3, k2tog, yo, k1 tbl, yo, [ssk, k1, k1 tbl, yo] twice, sk2p, yo, k1 tbl, k1, k2tog, yo, [k1 tbl, yo, ssk, k1] twice, k2.

Row 31: K2, k2tog, yo, k1 tbl, k1, [k1 tbl, yo, ssk, k1] 3 times, k2tog, yo, k1 tbl, [k1, k1 tbl, yo, ssk] twice, k2.

Row 33: [K1, k2tog, yo, k1 tbl] twice, yo, [ssk, k1, k1 tbl, yo] twice, sk2p, yo, k1 tbl, k1, k2tog, yo, [k1 tbl, yo, ssk, k1] twice.

Row 35: [K2tog, yo, k1 tbl, k1] twice, [k1 tbl, yo, ssk, k1] 3 times, k2tog, yo, k1 tbl, [k1, k1 tbl, yo, ssk] twice.

Row 37: K1, k1 tbl, yo, ssk, k1, k1 tbl, yo, sk2p, yo, k1 tbl, k1, k2tog, yo, k1 tbl, yo, [ssk, k1, k1 tbl, yo] twice, sk2p, yo, k1 tbl, k1, k2tog, yo, k1 tbl, k1.

Row 39: K2, [k1 tbl, yo, ssk, k1] twice, k2tog, yo, k1 tbl, [k1, k1 tbl, yo, ssk] 4 times, k2.

Row 41: K3, k1 tbl, yo, ssk, k1, k1 tbl, [k1, k2tog, yo, k1 tbl] twice, [yo, ssk, k1, k1 tbl] twice, k1, k2tog, yo, k1 tbl, k3.

Row 43: K4, k1 tbl, yo, ssk, k1, [k2tog, yo, k1 tbl, k1] twice, [k1 tbl, yo, ssk, k1] twice, k2tog, yo, k1 tbl, k4.

Row 45: K5, k1 tbl, yo, sk2p, yo, k1 tbl, yo, ssk, k1, k1 tbl, yo, sk2p, yo, k1 tbl, k1, k2tog, yo, k1 tbl, yo, sk2p, yo, k1 tbl, k5.

Row 47: K6, [k1 tbl, k1] twice, [k1 tbl, yo, ssk, k1] twice, k2tog, yo, k1 tbl, [k1, k1 tbl] twice, k6.

Row 49: K11, k1 tbl, yo, ssk, k1, k1 tbl, k1, k2tog, yo, k1 tbl, k11.

Row 51: K12, k1 tbl, yo, ssk, k1, k2tog, yo, k1 tbl, k12.

Row 53: K13, k1 tbl, yo, sk2p, yo, k1 tbl, k13.

Row 55: K14, [k1 tbl, k1] twice, k13.

Chart row numbers (right side, bottom to top): 1, 3, 5, 7, 9, 11, 13, 15, 17, 19, 21, 23, 25, 27, 29, 31, 33, 35, 37, 39, 41, 43, 45, 47, 49, 51, 53, 55

Chart column numbers (bottom): 31, 30, 29, 28, 27, 26, 25, 24, 23, 22, 21, 20, 19, 18, 17, 16, 15, 14, 13, 12, 11, 10, 9, 8, 7, 6, 5, 4, 3, 2, 1

Legend:

Symbol	Meaning	Symbol	Meaning
☐	Knit	△	SK2P
◯	Yarn over	⟋	K3tog
⟋	K2tog	℔	K1tbl
⟍	SSK		

HINTS AND TIPS

If knitting the Size S short sleeve version you will have 15g of yarn remaining. This yarn can be split in two to extend the sleeves for approx 10cm/4". For larger sizes and longer sleeves a second skein of yarn will be required.

SPECIAL INSTRUCTIONS

sssk slip, slip, slip, k (2st dec)
k3tog knit 3 together
slm slip marker

OLEUM SOCKS

by Rachel Coopey

ABBREVIATIONS

cdd	Centered double decrease. Slip 2 sts as if to k2tog, k1, pass the 2 slipped sts over
k	Knit
k2tog	Knit two stitches together as one stitch
kwise	Knitwise, as if to knit
p	Purl
pwise	Purlwise, as if to purl
p2tog	Purl two stitches together as one stitch
RS	Right side of work
sl	Slip the next stitch from left to right purl-wise.
ssk	Slip one stitch as if to knit, slip the next stitch as if to knit, insert left needle into front of these two stitches and knit them together.
st	Stitch
tbl	Through the back loop
WS	Wrong side of work
wyib	With yarn in back
wyif	With yarn in front

YARN
baa ram ewe Titus, shade: Aire; 1 x 100g skein

NEEDLES
2.5mm (UK 13-12/US 1-2) 80cm/32" circular needles or DPNs (or size needed to get gauge).

OTHER SUPPLIES
Cable needle; Stitchmarkers; Tapestry needle

GAUGE
36 sts x 50 rows = 10cm/4" over st st

SIZES
Small (Large)
To fit foot circumference: 18-20 (23-25.5) cm/7-8 (9-10)"

LEG LENGTH
15cm/6"

PATTERN NOTES
The charted stitch patterns are also given in written form at the end of the pattern.

PATTERN

CUFF

Cast on 60 (70) sts. Join to work in the round, being careful not to twist.
Place marker for start of round.
Rib round: *K3, p2, rep from * to end of round.
Last round sets rib pattern. Work this round 39 more times.
K1, this is the new start of the round, place a new marker.

LEG

Reading from right to left, or using written chart instructions, work rounds 1-22 of Chart A once then work rounds 1-15 once more (37 rounds).

HEEL FLAP

K3, turn work so WS is facing. Heel Flap will be worked back and forth on the next 30 (35) sts, beginning with a WS row. Keep remaining 30 (35) sts on needles for instep.
Row 1 (WS): Sl1 wyif, p29 (34).
Row 2 (RS): *Sl1 wyib, k1, rep from * to last st, k1.
Repeat these 2 rows 14 more times, then work row 1 once more.

TURN HEEL

Row 1 (RS): Sl1 wyib, k16 (19), ssk, k1, turn, leaving remaining 10 (12) sts unworked.
Row 2: Sl1 wyif, p5 (6), p2tog, p1, turn, leaving remaining 10 (12) sts unworked
Row 3: Sl1 wyib, k to 1 st before gap, ssk, k1, turn.
Row 4: Sl1 wyif, p to 1 st before gap, p2tog, p1, turn.
Repeat last 2 rows 4 (5) more times. All heel sts have been worked. 18 (21) heel sts remain.

GUSSET

Set-up Round: Sl 1, k17 (20), pick up and knit 16 sts along edge of heel flap (1 stitch in each slipped stitch along the edge of the flap), work across instep as foll: [P1, k3, p1] 6 (7) times. Pick up and knit 16 sts along edge of heel flap, k34 (37). Place marker for new start of round (at start of instep sts). 80 (88) stitches.
Round 1: Work in pattern as set across instep stitches, ssk, k to 2 sts before end of round, k2tog. 78 (86) sts.
Round 2: Work in pattern as set across instep stitches, k to end of round.
Last 2 rounds set pattern on instep and gusset decreases.
Repeat these 2 rounds 9 (8) more times. 60 (70) sts. You should now have 30 (35) sts on instep and sole.

FOOT

Work even in pattern as set (rib on instep and st st on sole) until sock measures 5cm/2" less than the desired foot length.

Round 1: Knit
Round 2: Purl
Work these 2 rounds once more, then work round 1 once more.

TOE

Round 1: Purl.
Round 2: K1, ssk, k24 (29), k2tog, k1, pm, k1, ssk, knit to last 3 sts, k2tog, k1. 56 (66) sts.
Round 3: Purl.
Round 4: *K1, ssk, k to 3 sts before marker, K2tog, k1, slm; repeat from * once more. 52 (62) sts.

Repeat last 2 rounds 8 (10) more times. 20 (22) sts.
Cut yarn, leaving a 30cm/12" tail. Graft sts together using Kitchener stitch. Weave in ends.

CHART A: WRITTEN INSTRUCTIONS

Round 1: Knit. (10 sts)
Round 2: Purl.
Rounds 3-4: Repeat rounds 1-2.
Round 5: K, yo, k3, cdd, k3, yo.
Round 6: K2, p7, k.
Round 7: K2, yo, k2, cdd, k2, yo, k.
Round 8: K3, p5, k2.
Round 9: K3, yo, k, cdd, k, yo, k2.
Round 10: Knit.
Round 11: K4, yo, cdd, yo, k3.
Round 12: Knit.
Round 13: Purl.
Rounds 14-15: Repeat rounds 12-13.
Round 16: Repeat round 5.
Round 17: P2, k7, p.
Round 18: Repeat round 7.
Round 19: P3, k5, p2.
Round 20: Repeat round 9.
Round 21: P4, k3, p3.
Round 22: Repeat round 11.

CHART A

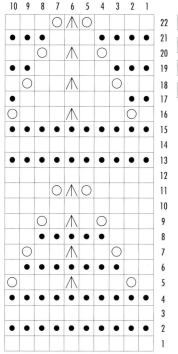

KEY

☐	Knit
●	Purl
○	Yarn over
⋀	Central double decrease

SEPTEMBER WRAP

by Julie Glaze

ABBREVIATIONS
UK crochet terms used throughout

ch	Chain
dc	Double Crochet
dtr	Double Treble
htr	Half Treble
lp(s)	Loop(s)
rep	Repeat
rnd	Round
sk	Skip
ss	Slip stitch
sp	Space
tr	Treble
trtr	Triple Treble

YARN
baa ram ewe Titus, shade: Yorkstone; 2 x 100g skeins

GAUGE
Single motif measures 8cm x 8cm / 3.25" x 3.25"
Crochet hook: 4mm (UK 8/US 6)

OTHER SUPPLIES
Brooch pin; Tapestry needle

SIZE
150cm wide x 24cm deep/59" wide x 9.5" deep

PATTERN NOTES
This pattern is for the improving crocheter and uses a variety of stitches and techniques to expand skills including a 'join-as-you-go' technique. Please ensure you read the pattern before starting.

PATTERN

Motif Set-up: 6ch, join with a ss in first ch (6th ch from hook) to form ring.

Rnd 1: 1ch, dc into ring, *6ch, 2dc into ring; rep from * a further 6 times, 6ch, dc into ring, ss in first dc, do not turn. (8 lps made)

Rnd 2: Ss in first ch of 6ch-lp on Rnd 1, ss in 2nd ch of 6ch-lp on Rnd 1, dc in same 6ch-lp, *8ch, sk next 6ch-lp, dc in next 6ch-lp; rep from * twice more, 8ch, sk next 6ch-lp, ss to first dc, do not turn. (4 lps formed)

Rnd 3: (2dc, 2htr, 2tr, 2dtr, 1trtr, 2dtr, 2tr, 2htr, 2dc) in each 8ch-lp around, ss in first dc, do not turn. (4 leaf bases formed)

Rnd 4: Ss in 2nd dc on Rnd 3, *dc in each of next 2htr, dc into tr, 3ch, ss in last dc (picot formed), dc into tr, dc in each of next 2dtr, (htr, tr, 2dtr, 3ch, ss in last dtr, dtr, tr, htr) all into trtr, dc in each of next 2dtr, dc in each of next 2tr, 3ch, ss in last dc (picot formed), dc in each of next 2htr, 2ch, sk 4dc; rep from * a further 3 times, ss in first dc on Rnd 4.

INSTRUCTIONS FOR JOINING MOTIFS AS-YOU-GO

Motifs are joined as you work Rnd 4 at every adjacent picot. If there is not a motif to join down one side, simply work the picot as set in Rnd 4.

Work join as follows: Complete first motif, then ensuring right side of work is facing up, substitute the 2nd ch of the 3ch-picot with ss into 3ch-picot of adjacent motif so the picot join is worked as follows: 1ch, ss into 3ch-picot on adjacent motif, 1ch.

When working ss into an adjoining motif, it helps to ensure that the yarn is taken behind the motifs and that the hook is inserted from the back to the front of the adjoining picot.

Make a total of 42 motifs and join-as-you-go follow the schematic for placement. All joining should worked in the same manner on 1, 2, 3 or 4 sides of the motif as required. It is suggested you start at the middle of the layout and work outwards rather than from end-to-end.

LEAFY PIN

Make 2 motifs without joining.

Make a treble circle backing as follows:

Rnd 1: 4ch, 11tr into 4th ch from hook (ch adjacent knot), ss in 3rd ch to join. (12 sts)

Rnd 2: 3ch, 2tr in each tr, ss in 3rd ch to join. (24 sts)

Place the 2 motifs on top of one another ensuring they are staggered and each of the intermediate picots are joined. Stitch the backing circle on to the rear and a brooch pin onto the backing circle.

SPECIAL INSTRUCTIONS

Double Treble (dtr): yarn over hook twice, pull up a loop (4 loops on hook), yarn over hook and pull through 2 loops on hook (3 loops now on hook), yarn over hook and pull through 2 loops on hook (2 loops now on hook), yarn over hook and pull through remaining 2 loops on hook (1 loop now on hook).

Triple Treble (trtr): yarn over hook 3 times, pull up a loop (5 loops on hook), yarn over hook and pull through 2 loops on hook (4 loops now on hook), yarn over hook and pull through 2 loops on hook (3 loops now on hook), yarn over hook and pull through 2 loops on hook (2 loops now on hook), yarn over hook and pull through remaining 2 loops on hook (1 loop now on hook).

SINGLE MOTIF

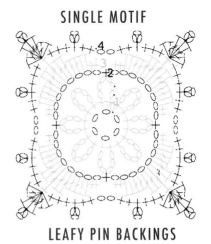

LEAFY PIN BACKINGS

KEY

0	ch	T	tr
·	ss	⌿	dtr
+	dc	⫽	trtr
T	htr		

JOINING MOTIFS

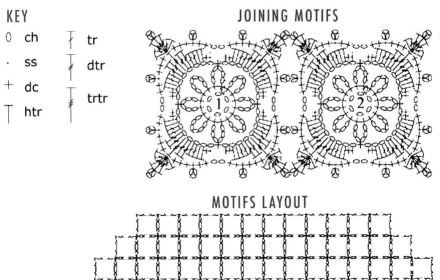

MOTIFS LAYOUT

STRIPING COWL

by Joy McMillan

ABBREVIATIONS

dpn	Double pointed needle(s)
MC	Main colour
CC	Contrast colour
pm	Place marker
rnd	Round

YARN

baa ram ewe Titus, MC shade: Eccup; 1 x 100g skein; CC shade: White Rose; 1 x 100g skein

GAUGE

23 sts x 26 rows = 10cm/4" measured over stocking stitch
Set of 3.5mm (UK9/US4) DPNs

OTHER SUPPLIES

Stitch marker
Waste yarn for provisional cast on
Darning needle for grafting
Spare DPN to hold grafting stitches

SIZE

To fit an adult. Finished cowl: 14cm deep x 150cm diameter / 5.5" x 59"

PATTERN NOTES

This pattern starts with a provisional cast on and is worked in the round, with the final live stitches grafted to the beginning giving a seamless join.
It does not matter which of the two yarns you start knitting with.
Call the first yarn you use MC and the second yarn CC.

PATTERN

With MC, cast on 60 stitches using a provisional cast on. Join to work in the rnd, being careful not to twist.
PM to mark beg of rnd.
Rnds 1-10: Using MC, knit.
Rnds 11-20: Using CC, knit.
Rep these last 20 rnds 18 more times (19 pairs of stripes worked).
Rep rnds 1-19 once more.

Break working yarn leaving a 90cm/35.5" tail. Use this to graft the two ends of the cowl together. Simply unravel the provisional cast on and put these live stitches onto a spare circular needle or DPNs. Block lightly, wear and enjoy.

SPECIAL INSTRUCTIONS

You can use any type of provisional cast on that you prefer. If you don't know how to do a provisional cast on, try popping it in your favourite search engine online.

DASHING DASCHUND

By Ella Austin

ABBREVIATIONS

beg	Beginning
CC	Contrast colour
cdd	Centred double decrease: slip 2 stitches knitwise together, knit 1, pass slipped stitches over
DPN	Double pointed needle(s)
k	Knit
kfb	Knit one through the front then through the back (same stitch)
k2tog	Knit two together
MC	Main colour
PM	Place marker
rnd	Round
ssk	Slip one knitwise, slip one purlwise, knit two slipped stitches together
sts	Stitches
w&t	Wrap and turn: bring the yarn to the front, slip 1 st purlwise, turn work. Bring yarn to front and slip 1 st purlwise.

YARN

baa ram ewe Titus in shades:
Parkin (MC) x 25g
Coal (CC1) x 5g
Filey (CC2) x 4g

GAUGE

16 sts x 18 rows = 5cm/2" measured on blocked colourwork section.
Set of 2mm (UK14 / US0) DPNs

SIZE

One size: 22cm/8.5" long, 9cm/3.5" tall

OTHER SUPPLIES

2 buttons for eyes; tapestry needle; 1 stitchmarker; scrap yarn; toy stuffing

PATTERN NOTES

Casting on: use a cable cast on method to create a firm cast on edge. Leave long tails when casting on for the legs, ears and tail. You can use the long ends to sew the parts together. If you are not sure how to do i-cord or grafting (sometimes called Kitchener stitch), try popping them in your favourite search engine online.

PATTERN

NOSE

With CC1 and using cable cast on method, cast on 8 sts (see notes). Divide evenly between dpns and join to work in the rnd, being careful not to twist. PM to mark beg of rnd.

Rnds 1-3: Knit 3 rnds.

Switch to MC.

HEAD

Rnd 4: *Kfb; rep from * to end. 16 sts

Rnd 5: Knit.

Rnd 6: Knit.

Rnd 7: K5, kfb, k3, kfb, k to end. 18 sts

Rnd 8: Knit.

Rnd 9: K6, kfb, k3, kfb, k to end. 20 sts

Rnd 10: Knit.

Rnd 11: K7, kfb, k3, kfb, k to end. 22 sts

Rnd 12: Knit.

Rnd 13: K8, kfb, k3, kfb, k to end. 24 sts

Rnds 14-18: Knit 5 rnds.

Rnd 19: K8, kfb, kfb, k3, kfb, kfb, k to end. 28 sts

Rnd 20: Knit.

Rnd 21: K9, kfb, kfb, k5, kfb, kfb, k to end. 32 sts

Rnd 22: Knit.

Rnd 23: K10, kfb, kfb, k7, kfb, kfb, k to end. 36 sts

Rnds 24-28: Knit 4 rnds.

START OF SHORT ROW SHAPING FOR BACK OF HEAD:

Rnd 29: K24 w&t .

Rnd 30: P12, w&t.

Rnd 31: K15 picking up wrap along the way, w&t

Rnd 32: P18, picking up wrap along the way, w&t.

Rnd 33: K to end of rnd, picking up wrap along the way.

Rnd 34: Knit, picking up wrap along the way.
Rnd 35: K27, w&t.
Rnd 36: P18, w&t.
Rnd 37: K15, w&t.
Rnd 38: P12, w&t.
Rnd 39: K to end of rnd, picking up wraps along the way.
Rnd 40: Knit, picking up wraps along the way.

NECK

Rnd 41: K11, cdd, k8, cdd, k to end. 32 sts
Rnd 42: Knit.
Rnd 43: K10, cdd, k6, cdd, k to end. 28 sts
Rnd 44: Knit.
Rnd 45: Kfb, kfb, k7, cdd, k4, cdd, k6, kfb, kfb, k1.
Rnd 46: Knit.
Rnd 47: Kfb, kfb, k to last 3 sts, kfb, kfb, k1. 32 sts
Rnds 48-55: Rep these last 2 rnds 4 more times. 48 sts

BODY

Rnds 56-58: Knit 3 rnds.
Rnds 59-94: Follow Colourwork Chart.
Rnds 95-99: Using MC, knit 5 rnds.

At this stage sew in all ends from the colourwork section and from working the dog's nose.
Transfer sts to scrap yarn, ensuring that beg of rnd is marked. Block the colourwork section by soaking it in cool water and leaving flat to dry. When the knitting is completely dry, stuff the head, neck and part of the body.

BOTTOM

Place sts held on scrap yarn back onto dpns and replace marker for beg of rnd.
Rnd 100: K2, cdd, k14, cdd, k4, cdd, k14, cdd, k2. 40 sts
Rnds 101-102: Knit 2 rnds.
Rnd 103: K1, cdd, k12, cdd, k2, cdd, k12, cdd, k1. 32 sts
Rnd 104: Knit.
Rnd 105: Cdd, k10, cdd, cdd, k10, cdd. 24 sts

Rearrange the sts so that the first 12 sts are on one needle and the remaining 12 on another. Stuff the rest of the body and graft the bottom closed.

LEGS
Make 4 the same

With MC cast on 14 sts (see notes). Divide evenly between dpns and join to work in the rnd, being careful not to twist.
Rnds 1-8: Knit 8 rnds.
Rnd 9: K5, kfb, k1, kfb, k to end. 16 sts
Rnd 10: K6, kfb, k1, kfb, k to end. 18 sts
Rnd 11: K7, kfb, k1, kfb, k to end. 20 sts
Rnds 12-14: Knit 3 rnds.
Rnd 15: K2tog, k4, [k2tog] 4 times, k4, k2tog. 14 sts
Rnd 16: Knit
Graft the bottom of the feet closed.

TAIL

With MC cast on 5 sts (see notes).
Work i-cord for 8cm/3".
Cut yarn and pull through all sts to close.

EARS
Make 2 the same

With MC cast on 10 sts (see notes).
Divide over 2 dpns and use a 3rd dpn to knit with (as you would for a toe up sock).
Join to work in the rnd.
Rnds 1-3: Knit 3 rnds.
Rnd 4: Kfb, k to last 2 sts, kfb, k1. 12 sts
Rnd 5: Knit.
Rnds 6-11: Rep last 2 rnds 3 times more. 18 sts
Rnds 12-13: Knit 2 rnds.
Rnd 14: Ssk, k to last 2 sts, k2tog. 16 sts
Rnd 15: Knit.
Rnds 16-21: Rep last 2 rnds 3 times more. 10 sts
Rnd 22: Ssk, k1, k2tog, ssk, k1, k2tog. 6 sts
Cut yarn and pull through all sts to close.

FINISHING
Use photos as a guide for finishing.
Stuff the legs and attach them to the body. It may take a few attempts to get the positions right, so don't weave in the ends until all 4 legs are sewn on and the dog can stand up on its own.
Sew the tail at the top of the dog's bottom.
Sew the ears at the back of the head.
Sew on button eyes.
(**Note:** for children under 3 it is recommended to use felt or sewn on eyes, as buttons can be a choking hazard.)
Sew the end of the nose closed.
Weave in all ends.

KEY

Parkin (MC)
Coal (CC1)
Filey (CC2)

CHART

DECEMBER HAT

by Kelly Herdrich

ABBREVIATIONS

beg	Beginning
CN	Cable needle
C6F	Cable 6 forwards: sl 3 sts onto CN, hold in front, K3 from LH needle, K3 from CN
DPN	Double-pointed needle(s)
k	Knit
kfb	Knit through the front then through the back of the same stitch
k2tog	Knit two together
LH	Left hand
p	Purl
pm	Place marker
rem	Remaining
rep	Repeat
rm	Remove marker
rnd	Round
sl	Slip
sm	Slip marker
st	Stitch

YARN

baa ram ewe Titus, shade: Crucible; 1 x 100g skein

GAUGE

25 sts x 32 rows = 10cm/4" using larger needles and measured over December Cable Panel after blocking or lightly stretched
Sets of 2.5mm (UK13-12 / US1-2) and 3.25mm (UK10 / US3) DPNs

OTHER SUPPLIES

Stitch markers
Cable needle

SIZE

Adult S (L) (approximately 48 (54)cm / 19 (21)" circumference)

PATTERN
With smaller needles, cast on 120 (136) sts. Join to work in the rnd, being careful not to twist.
PM to mark beg of rnd.

Rnd 1: *K2, p2; rep from * to end.
Rep last rnd 11 more times.

BODY
Switch to larger needles.

Rnd 13 (set-up rnd): SM, k2, p2, k2, p2, k6, p2, k3, p2, k6, p2, k2, p2, k2, p2, pm, k to last 2 sts, p2.
Rnd 14: Work row 1 of December Cable Panel between markers, sm, k to last 2 sts, p2.
Continue to work December Cable Panel between markers as set.

Rnds 15-43: Work next row of December Cable Panel, k to last 2 sts, p2.

SIZE S
Skip to rnd 56.

SIZE L
Rnds 44-55: Work next row of December Cable Panel, k to last 2 sts, p2.

CROWN
Rnd 56: Work row 1 of December Cable Panel, k to last 2 sts, p2.
Rnd 57: Work row 2 of December Cable Panel, *k6, k2tog; rep from * to last 3 sts, k1, p2. 110 (124) sts
Rnd 58: Work row 3 of December Cable Panel, k to last 2 sts, p2.
Rnd 59: Work row 4 of December Cable Panel, *k5, k2tog; rep from * to last 3 sts, k1, p2. 100 (112) sts
Rnd 60: Work row 5 of December Cable Panel, k to last 2 sts, p2.
Rnd 61: Work row 6 of December Cable Panel, *k4, k2tog; rep from * to last 3 sts, k1, p2. 90 (100) sts
Rnd 62: Work row 1 of December Cable Panel, k to last 2 sts, p2.
Rnd 63: Work row 2 of December Cable Panel, rm, *k3, k2tog; rep from * to last 3 sts, k1, p2. 80 (88) sts
Rnd 64: K1, *k2, k2tog; rep from * to last 3 sts, k2, sl1, rm, sl st back to LH needle, k2tog, pm. 60 (66) sts
Rnd 65: *K2tog; rep from * to end of rnd. 30 (33) sts
Rnd 66: *K2tog; rep from * to last 2(3) sts, k2tog, k0(1). 15 (17) sts
Cut yarn, leaving a 15cm/6" tail, pull through rem sts tightly. Weave in ends. Block gently and lay flat to dry.

SPECIAL INSTRUCTIONS

DECEMBER CABLE PANEL
Worked over 37 sts
Rnds 1-4: K2, p2, k2, p2, k6, p2,
k3, p2, k6, p2, k2, p2, k2, p2
Rnd 5: K2, p2, k2, p2, k6, p2, k1,
kfb, k1, p2, k6, p2, k2, p2, k2, p2
Rnd 6: K2, p2, k2, p2, C6F, p2,
k2tog, yo, k2tog, p2, C6F, p2, k2,
p2, k2, p2

KEY

☐	Knit
•	Purl
╱	K2tog
○	Yarn over
∨	Knit fb
◤━━◥	C6F

CHART

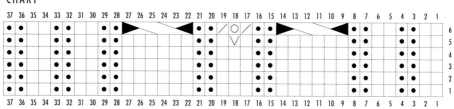

THANKS

As always there are so many people to thank for the creation of this book, many of whom will be unseen by the reader.

First, huge thanks to British hand-dyer **Joy McMillan**, aka The Knitting Goddess. Our 12 month range of one-off overdyed 'Titus Goddess' yarns led us to commission these designs from some of our favourite UK-based designers, many of whom were recommended by her. She is a legend.

Thanks too, of course, to **the wonderful designers** showcased in this book. We've squealed with excitement each time a new sample has arrived in the post, and it has been a pleasure and a privilege to work with each of you.

Enormous thanks to **Nic Blackmore** for making this book. It has been our first project working with Nic but it sure as hell won't be the last! Thanks also to our crochet tech editor **Rachel Atkinson**, who is always a joy to work with.

We are so grateful to all our lovely models who braved the harsh Yorkshire climate to pose for us: **Ruby, Katherine, Alice, James and Sarah** you are all beautiful!

And finally, where would we be without the most amazing team on the planet? There are no words to describe the marvellous group of people who dedicate so much time and effort as part of team **baa ram ewe**.

Katherine Johnson: you need a holiday! Katherine has worked tirelessly on this project and never dropped a ball. She is amazing.

Joelle Trousdale: your photography skills make us weak at the knees and this book would be a shadow of itself without them.

Alison Moreton: your eagle eye for detail never ceases to amaze us. We would be utterly lost without you.

Janet Welby-Jenkins: those fancy women's magazines don't know what they're missing – fabulous graphic design work, lady!

Jane Brumwell: quietly and patiently organised many additional samples, which all appeared just when we needed them and **Graeme Knowles-Miller** designed those beautiful Staysail mitts. We are spoiled rotten.

TITUS MINI KNITS

First published in 2015 by baa ram ewe © Copyright baa ram ewe 2015 All rights reserved.
All images in this publication © copyright baa ram ewe 2015

Printed by The Printing House, UK.

British Library Cataloguing in Publication Data: A catalogue record for this book is available from the British Library. ISBN-978-0-9927730-1-4